Dashing
LIFE STORIES
30-Day Devotional

Dying to Achieve Success and Happiness IN God

ELESHA STOREY

Disclaimer: It is not intended for this book to provide more than anecdotal information. Understand the author is not engaged in rendering professional advice of any kind.

No part of this book may be reproduced or transmitted in any form or by any means, electronic or mechanical, including photocopying, recording, or by any information storage or retrieval system, without permission in writing from the author/publisher except as provided by U.S. copyright law.

Names: Storey, Elesha, author.

Title: Dashing Life Stories 30-Day Devotional: Dying to Achieve Success and Happiness IN God

(Includes biblical references)

Description: 1st edition/Frisco Texas/My Storey Publishing

Paperback ISBN 13: 978-1-7362234-2-0

eBook ISBN 13: 978-1-7362234-5-1

Subjects: Non-fiction / Christian / Spirituality

Classification: Christian Life

Copyright ©2020 Elesha Storey. All rights reserved. Printed in the United States of America for worldwide distribution.

To order, go to:
https://www.dashingapparel.com or
https://www.dashingnation.org

My Storey Publishing
8745 Gary Burns Drive, Suite 160-153
Frisco, TX 75034

Contents

Dedication 7
With Thanks 8
Introduction 9

Week 1
Dashing Faith

Day 1: ***Decide*** - But I Don't Want To Get My Hair Wet 11

Day 2: ***Attest*** - Confession Is Good For The Soul 13

Day 3: ***Salvation*** - Better Saved Than Sorry 15

Day 4: ***Hope*** - God Bless The United Skates Of America 17

Day 5: ***Invite*** - My Invitation Must Have Gotten Lost In The Mail 19

Day 6: ***New*** - You Give Me Butterflies 21

Day 7: ***Give*** - Giving Just Enough For The City 23

Week 2
Dashing Relationship

Day 8: ***Dwell*** - Long Distance Textlationship 25

Day 9: ***Assemble*** - We Are The Titans 29

Day 10: *Sin* - The Devil Made Me Do It 33

Day 11: *Heart* - B-Side Girl 35

Day 12: *Intimacy* - Break 2912, You Got Your Ears On? Come Back? 37

Day 13: *Naked* - Naked As A J-Bird 39

Day 14: *Gratitude* - Throw Your Hands In The Air And Praise Him Like You Just Don't Care 41

Week 3
Dashing Growth

Day 15: *Develop* - Photo Finish 43

Day 16: *Adhere* - The Ten Suggestions 45

Day 17: *Scripture* - Sticks And Stones 49

Day 18: *Holy Spirit* - We Got Spirit! Yes We Do! We Got Spirit! How About You? 53

Day 19: *Identity* - Witness Protection Program 57

Day 20: *Nor'easter* - Winds Of Change 61

Day 21: *Grace* - The Gift That Keeps On Giving 65

Week 4
Dashing Purpose

Day 22: *Decrease* - Tweener Blues 69

Day 23: *Authority* - VIP Seating 71

Day 24: *Serve* - CrossWord Puzzle 77

Day 25: *History* - I Have No Spades And Only One Face Card 81

Day 26: *Incubation* - The WIIFM In The Wait 85

Day 27: *Next Chapter* - Cliff Notes And A Cliff Hanger 89

Day 28: *Gifts* - If The Present Fits, I Must Re-Gift 91

Week 5
Dashing Forward

Day 29: *Dash* - White Knuckles And A Tailwind 95

Day 30: *Ing* - Verb 99

About the Author 101

Dedication

I dedicate this book to my Heavenly Father, who loved me before I knew Him—who brought me through the changes, trials, challenges, triumphs, miracles, and victories that made me the woman I am today. I also dedicate this book to my Lord and Savior, Jesus Christ. Without his unselfish love and sacrifice, I would not be here today. Lastly, I dedicate this book to my earthly father, Elijah Storey, my first love and hero. His passing was the catalyst for my ***Dashing Journey***. God planned that he should go so that I could *dash*.

With Thanks

To my mom (Peggy Storey), my sister (Vicki), my brother (Michael), and my son (David), "Thank you."

You were and are my True North, the constants who were there for me through it all: no money, no job, no matter what.
I love you.

To my friends and family who gave me love, support, encouragement and would not let me quit,
I love and thank you too.

To all my supporters who I don't personally know but who continued to show me love, I appreciate you so very much.

Last but not least, thank you to those who have embraced the movement and are truly Dashing for life.

Introduction

Thank you for taking this **Dashing Journey** with me. I pray that by sharing my *Storey*, you are inspired to do your Dash.

I lost my Dad on April 13, 2015. He had a great homegoing service with over 500 people in attendance. After the graveside ceremony, I took some of his flowers and put them on the graves of family members buried nearby. I placed them on the graves of my great-grandparents, who I was blessed to have known and loved, as well as my great-uncle and grandmother. While doing this, I kept looking at the dashes between their dates of birth and death. I thought to myself, *what a small representation of such grand and awesome people.*

Days after, I could not stop thinking about that dash. If I wanted to please God, live my purpose, and see Him and my loved ones again, I needed to change mine. Then God dropped *DASHING* into my spirit—Dying to Achieve Success and Happiness IN God. The D stands for Dying. When you want to do something very badly, you are dying to do it. To be like Christ, you must die to self and the flesh, and as we age, we are all dying daily. ASH is Achieve Success and Happiness. The abundant life promised by God, which looks different for everyone, can only be achieved when you are IN connection with God.

Through my earthly father's death, my Heavenly Father turned tragedy into victory. The victory was finding my life's calling to inspire and help others find their purpose and live a *Dashing Life*.

I pray this devotional makes you think, laugh, reminisce, and move closer to God. It can and should be re-read monthly. Why? Because every day is a *Faith* walk, and having a *Relationship* with God that is consistently *Growing* will reveal your *Purpose* and move you *Forward* to your *Dashing Life*.

Week 1
Dashing Faith

Day 1

Decide

But I Don't Want To Get My Hair Wet

I was raised in a Baptist Church. New believers got baptized as the sign of their decision to become a Christian and all that choice entails, hence the title Baptist Church. I made my choice at age 13, but when it came time for me to get baptized, I almost changed my mind. You see, I had made the decision a couple of weeks earlier and was more than ready then, but now, I had just gotten my hair done. *I don't want my cute new hairdo ruined by getting it wet,* I thought to myself. *And even if I wear a swim cap,*

Dashing Life Stories

my edges will still get wet! The decision I had made a couple of weeks earlier was clashing with the choice I needed to make that day.

"But if serving the Lord seems undesirable to you, then choose for yourselves this day whom you will serve, whether the gods your ancestors served beyond the Euphrates or the gods of the Amorites, in whose land you are living. But as for me and my household, we will serve the Lord" (Joshua 24:15, NIV).

Deciding to serve the Lord is not a one-time event. It is a daily choice that sometimes does not go along with our current circumstances, perceived or real. Either recently or some time ago, you professed your faith in God and your belief in Jesus Christ, but your current actions may say differently. Is there something or someone hindering your daily walk with God? Could it be what you are reading, watching, or who you are spending time with? Maybe it's time to make some changes.

Let us decide today to **Live In Faith Every** day by renewing our minds, our faith, and our commitment to follow Jesus daily.

"Father God, please give me the strength and courage to start each day with and for You. And the wisdom to make daily decisions that honor You in order to continue *dashing* for Your Kingdom here on earth and in heaven. In Jesus' name. Amen."

Week 1
Dashing Faith
Day 2

*A*ttest

Confession Is Good For The Soul

I moved away from home in my mid-20s and struggled to find a church I could call home. I visited several churches searching for the right fit. During one of my visits to a well-established Baptist Church, the pastor asked if anyone wanted to come upfront and give a testimony. Several people took the opportunity. However, this one lady who was obviously mad did not give a testimony but put her husband on blast. She told the entire church she knew her husband was cheating. To me, it was kind of funny, but I'm sure not to them. It would have been better for him if he had confessed to her before she found out and saved himself from judgment and embarrassment.

"That if you confess with your mouth Jesus *as* Lord and believe in your heart that God raised Him from the dead, you will be saved" (Romans 10:9, NASB).

God only requires two things for us to be saved; one of them is confession. We often put off confessing because we feel it is uncomfortable, unwarranted, or we have time to do it later. The embarrassed man at church was more than likely waiting for the perfect time to tell his wife about his indiscretion. Subsequently, he waited too late to confess and suffered the consequences.

If you believe Jesus is Lord, died and rose from the dead and have not voiced that, what are you waiting for? Are you embarrassed or afraid of what others will say or think of you? Do you have doubts, or are you just shy? Whatever your reason, please do not wait too long.

Once you have confessed your belief and faith in Jesus Christ, you must continue to profess it so that your actions and words reflect your faith. You need to do this not only to be saved but to save others.

"Lord Jesus, You paid the ultimate price to save me. Words cannot express my gratitude. I stand ready to tell the world of my belief in You and about this marvelous thing You have done. Thank You for who You are, what You have done, are doing, and will do in my life. I give You praise, honor, and glory for it all. Amen."

Week 1
Dashing Faith
Day 3

Salvation

Better Saved Than Sorry

Like I said on Day 1, I was raised in a Baptist Church, St. John Missionary Baptist Church, to be exact. Just about my entire extended family on my mother's side attended St. John. My great-uncles and aunts, great-grandparents, and grandparents were all church leaders. They were my real-life examples of Bible prophets, especially my maternal grandmother. When I was about 12 years old, we had a conversation about being saved. I asked her, "Isn't it selfish to follow Jesus just to be saved?"

"The fear of the Lord is the beginning of wisdom, And the knowledge of the Holy One is understanding" (Proverbs 9:10, NKJV).

My decision to put my faith and belief in Jesus Christ may have started as a reaction to fear and self-preservation; however, my grandmother taught me that was okay. God often puts us in scary, uncomfortable, and dependent situations to get our attention so that He can save us. Think about what is going on in your life right now. Have you found yourself in situations where you have failed, been frightened, or frustrated? Is God trying to get your attention? If you died today, where would you spend eternity?

Regardless of the catalyst that prompts us to believe in the death and resurrection of Jesus Christ as the Son of God, salvation is ours when we do. That's Good News!

"Father God, thank You for getting my attention. Thank You for loving me first and loving me still. Please continue to give us all undeserved grace, mercy, protection, forgiveness, and love. All this I ask in the mighty name of Jesus Christ, my risen Lord and Savior. Amen."

Week 1
Dashing Faith
Day 4

*H*ope

God Bless The United Skates Of America

When I was about 15 years old, I would go skating at United Skates of America (USA) on Sunday nights. The only way I could do that was to attend church on Sunday mornings. My mom would say, "If you don't go to church, you don't get to go skating." I loved to go roller skating on Sunday! In fact, I met my first boyfriend at USA. Before we officially met, I would see him staring at me. I was too shy to say anything but would occasionally glance back at him. I couldn't wait to get out of church, have dinner, and get to the skating rink. I trusted that my mom would keep her word and let me go if I did my part. I hoped he would be there, and I knew he hoped I would be there too.

"Now faith is the substance of things hoped for, the evidence of things not seen" (Hebrews 11:1, NKJV).

Hope, faith, and trust go hand-in-hand. You cannot have one without the other two. Faith is defined as having confidence or trust in a person or thing, and hope is an optimistic attitude of mind based on an expectation or desire. Faith says it is so now, and hope says—in the future—it can be.

We put our hope and trust in so many things other than God, like our jobs, bank accounts, people, and other earthly possessions. It is not enough to just believe *in* God; you must *believe* God. You have to hope, trust, and believe that what He says is true.

What are you hoping for today? Who or what are you trusting for the thing you hope will come to pass? Try putting your hope and trust in a God who never changes and never fails. He is the same yesterday, today, and tomorrow.

"Dear Lord, today is all I have, and You are all I need. My present and future are in Your hands, and I trust them with You. My hope and prayers are that my desires align with Yours so that my *dash* will count. Thank You for a life filled with hope and possibility. In Jesus' name, I pray, Amen."

Week 1
Dashing Faith
Day 5

*I*nvite

My Invitation Must Have Gotten Lost In The Mail

I went to a large high school with over 5,000 students. I was not really part of the in-crowd, nor was I part of the so-called outcasts. I was comfortably in the middle with no alliance or ties to either side. I knew the right people in both groups, and the right people in both groups knew me. It was working for me for a while until one day…

One person from each group was having a party on the same night. I just knew I would have to choose which party to attend. However, by the night of the parties, I had not received an invitation from either. That night, I was home alone, wishing I had invited some of them into my life.

"I know your deeds, that you are neither cold nor hot. I wish you were either one or the other! So, because you are lukewarm—neither hot nor cold—I am about to spit you out of my mouth" (Revelation 3:15-16, NIV).

Relationships are work. In them, you risk being hurt, but the benefits outweigh the risks. I found that out the hard way. By playing it safe, being lukewarm, and not building relationships on either side, I was left out in the cold.

God does not force Himself on us. He invites us to have a relationship with Him with the benefits that come with that relationship. Jesus died so that you can have a direct relationship with Him and our Heavenly Father.

The Bible is full of invitations from Him. It tells of the abundant benefits of having faith in God. It also speaks of the consequences of not. Are you lukewarm with one foot in the world and the other in the Word? Jesus is calling you. "Come," he said. Then Peter got down out of the boat, walked on the water and came toward Jesus" (Matthew 14:29, NIV). Won't you accept His invitation today? Come on in, the water's fine!

"Dear Heavenly Father, thank You for inviting me into relationship with You. By faith, I am stepping out of the boat of worldly tepidness, out of the boat of fear and doubt, and into the water of a *Dashing Life*. In Jesus' name, Hallelujah and Amen."

Week 1
Dashing Faith
Day 6

New

You Give Me Butterflies

I was labeled a "tomboy" growing up. There was nothing "girly" about me. I climbed trees, fought boys, and hung out with my dad in the garage. Around age 14, things started to change. I was physically, emotionally, and mentally developing into a woman. I no longer wanted to climb trees, fight boys, or hang out in the garage. I started to dress differently, talk differently, had different interests, different friends, went to a different school, and hung out in different places — and boys started to notice me. The "tomboy" caterpillar was turning into a beautiful butterfly. Not only did boys begin to notice me, but I also began to notice them.

Each time I saw one boy, in particular, I suddenly felt nervous and excited. He gave me butterflies.

"Therefore, if anyone *is* in Christ, *he is* a new creation; old things have passed away; behold, all things have become new" (2 Corinthians 5:17, NKJV).

Change is usually not easy. My tomboy to teen girl transformation was called adolescence. The physical, emotional, and mental changes wreaked havoc on me and everyone near me; just ask my parents. The same can be said for the caterpillar to butterfly transformation. The caterpillar must go into a dark cocoon for some time and then struggles to get out before it emerges as a beautiful butterfly.

Becoming a new creature in Christ is not easy, either. You can't do some things you used to do, go some places you used to go, watch some things you used to watch, read some things you used to read, or hang with some people you used to hang with. Eventually, you don't want to. God will give you new things to do, read, and watch, and new places to go with new people to *dash* with.

"Dear Heavenly Father, thank You for reconciliation, restoration, and justification through Jesus Christ. I pray that I walk in this newness of life excited and so in love with Jesus that He gives me butterflies. I pray this in His mighty name. Amen."

Week 1
Dashing Faith
Day 7

Give

Giving Just Enough For The City

Growing up, one of my favorite artists was Stevie Wonder. I felt his songs made you think and wonder—thus, the name *Stevie Wonder*. I have always been a deep thinker, and to me, his name had nothing to do with him being able to play the keyboard without sight. I even joined his fan club. However, all I did was join. I did not go to his concerts, and I did not buy an album. My siblings did, so I listened to theirs. I did not go to fan club events. I did not read the club rules and bylaws, nor did I respond to fan club correspondence. I never made an effort to participate. So, was I really a fan or a fan of being a fan?

Dashing Life Stories

"For as the body without the spirit is dead, so faith without works is dead also" (James 2:26, NKJV).

The Bible says we are saved by grace and faith in Jesus Christ. So, does that absolve us from doing anything beyond having faith? God gives us time, talents, money, and other resources to use in His service, for His glory and our good. Who knows how much good I could have done if I would have actually gotten involved in the fan club and gone beyond deep thinking into deeper service? Who knows how much it could have benefited me? Maybe I would have gotten to meet Stevie Wonder in person. Wouldn't that have been something?

One of my favorite Stevie Wonder songs is "Living Just Enough for the City." This song tells the story of people barely getting by with just enough to make it. Are you giving just enough of your time, talents, and resources to be called a fan of God? Isn't it time for you to move from a fan of God to a child of God? He is waiting for you to put feet to your faith. Once you do, God will multiply your efforts to accomplish more than you can imagine.

"Heavenly Father, I apologize for my just enough faith. You said in Your Word that if my brother or sister is in need of food and clothing, prayer is not enough. If we are able, we are supposed to help them. In the same way, faith alone is not enough. Please give me an opportunity to move from fan to family, from being blessed to being a blessing, and from just enough to more than enough. All this I ask in Jesus' name. Amen."

Week 2
Dashing Relationship
Day 8

D*well*

Long Distance Textlationship

When I was in my 30s, I met a guy at work that I really liked. We would spend break time and lunch together every day. After three months on the job, I was transferred to another department, so our daily interactions ceased. I ran into him a month later in the breakroom. He told me that he missed me and wanted to get to know me better with the intent of moving toward a committed relationship. I was thrilled and ready for the journey but by month five, no progress. We did not see each other at work because we were not in the same department. We did not see each other outside of work because we lived an hour apart. We exchanged text messages but rarely had voice calls. How could we have built a relationship without spending time together? I became disillusioned and wrote him off.

"Abide in Me, and I in you. As the branch cannot bear fruit of itself, unless it abides in the vine, neither can you, unless you abide in Me" (John 15:4, NKJV).

It was obvious that my work crush was just that—a crush. It was a surface level infatuation based on limited interaction. Had he taken the time to go past the superficial and really gotten to know me, our budding relationship could have blossomed into marriage, children, businesses, or even ministries; only God knows. A year later, I ran into him, and he told me he regretted his inaction, that I was the one who got away, and he missed out.

Building a relationship with Jesus requires spending TIME. With Him, the **T**ransforming **I**nteraction **M**eans **E**verything. As you dwell in Him, He will begin to dwell in you. In other words, He will take residence in your heart and mind, changing and developing you to bear the fruit of your purpose.

Your relationship with Him can't reach its full potential (bear fruit) without a consistent connection. It will wither, die, and eventually get cut off. Don't be the one who misses out, the one who withers and dies without the Vine. Start spending consistent quality time with Jesus. The fruit you will bear and the harvest you receive will be **time** well spent.

"Father God, You are the Gardener, and Jesus is the Vine. As You tend to the Vine, You are tending to me. I pray that I come to know You better through knowing the Vine and that my transformation yields a harvest here on earth and in Your eternal Kingdom. I pray this in Jesus' name. Amen."

Week 2
Dashing Relationship
Day 9

Assemble

We Are The Titans

My high school had 11 buildings and 5,000 students. It was like a small college campus. Because the school was so big, it was easy for students to form smaller groups and disconnect from the larger student body. To address this issue, the school held periodic mandatory assemblies. These assemblies provided instruction, announcements, and other pertinent information. They provided an opportunity to learn, fellowship, encourage, and support each other. They often ended in a prep rally to inspire us and remind us of who we were and what we were capable of. They also set the tone for that day and the week ahead. The call and response went like this:

> Everywhere we go
>
> People want to know
>
> Who we are
>
> So, we tell them
>
> We are the Titans!
>
> The Mighty, Mighty Titans!

"Not neglecting to meet together, as is the habit of some, but encouraging one another, and all the more as you see the Day approaching" (Hebrew 10:25, NRSV).

As a freshman, I was excited about the assemblies. In my sophomore year, they began to seem like a chore. My junior year was full of so much activity that I didn't have time to attend, so I stopped going.

Have you stopped going to church? Have you stopped assembling with other believers? The Bible says we should not miss coming together for a reason. There is strength, power, comfort, safety, and growth in the assembly of believers. God knows that, and so does the enemy, which is why he sends distractions and negative thoughts your way to keep you isolated. Spending time with God and other believers will help you stay ready today and in the days to come.

Dashing Relationship

"Dear Lord Jesus, I ask for Your grace for the continued assembly of believers. I pray that the more we come together, the brighter Your light will shine through us. So much so that everywhere we go, people will want to know who we are, so we can tell them about a Father who loves them, about Jesus, and who we are in Him. We are followers of Christ. Mighty, Mighty Christians! I pray this in Your mighty name, Hallelujah and Amen."

Week 2
Dashing Relationship
Day 10

Sin
The Devil Made Me Do It

Flip Wilson was a comedian who had his own variety show in the early 1970s. I used to love it when he played the female character, Geraldine Jones. In one skit, Geraldine was the wife of the pastor of "The Church of What's Happening Now." She had bought yet another dress, and the pastor asked her why she bought a dress she didn't need. Geraldine said, "The devil made me do it." She explained that the devil complimented her, pushed her into the dressing room, tore off her clothes, put the dress on her, pulled out a gun, and forced her to write a check. In each skit where Geraldine got caught doing something wrong, she blamed it on the devil.

"No one who lives in him keeps on sinning. No one who continues to sin has either seen him or known him" (1 John 3:6, NIV).

If Geraldine were a real person, her continuing to do wrong, not taking responsibility, and not changing would eventually harm her relationship with her husband. We are all human, and per the Word, "we all fall short." However, forgiveness after repentance requires a positive change to sustain the relationship.

Sin is a barrier between you and God. It must be removed to know and stay close to Him. Jesus died to remove that barrier so that we can have a relationship with Him and the Father. Are you putting that barrier back brick by brick, sin by sin? Are you sabotaging your relationship with God and blaming it on the devil? It's time to stop building and nurturing your relationship with sin and start building and nurturing one with the Savior.

"Lord Jesus, thank You for opening the door to having a direct relationship with You and the Father. I am sorry for taking your sacrifice for granted. I am sorry for my perpetual cycles of sin, empty-gesture repentance, sin, and repeat. I pray the door You opened does not close before I step through. Today, I take a step forward in building an authentic relationship with You and the Father, and no one is making me do it. I pray this in your precious name. Amen."

Week 2
Dashing Relationship
Day 11

*H*eart

B-Side Girl

I have been labeled a "B-side" girl. I'm called that because I usually like the B-side of an album more than the A-side with all the popular songs heard on the radio. Consequently, I sing and talk about songs most people never heard of. However, they are missing out. Some of the best love songs are B-side songs. Songs like "Love You Anyway" by Cameo, which is about loving someone even if they don't love you back.

"For I am persuaded that neither death nor life, nor angels nor principalities nor powers, nor things present nor things to

come, nor height nor depth, nor any other created thing, shall be able to separate us from the love of God which is in Christ Jesus our Lord" (Romans 8:38-39, NKJV).

My B-side songs are unpopular and unknown because most don't go past the feel-good surface level songs on side A. The same can be said for relationships; some are not deeper because one or both parties don't go past the surface *like* to experience deeper *love*.

The Cameo song is an excellent illustration of the relationship between God and some of us. His love is unconditional; our love is not. His love is on the B-side—in this world but not of it. Our love is on the A-side, worldly and popular. We say we love God, but do we really? If this is you, how long are you going to continue your one-sided relationship with Him? Join the B-side; open your heart and let Him in.

"Dear Heavenly Father, thank You for continuing to hold my hand even when I let go of Yours. Thank You for loving me first and loving me still. Thank You for loving me when I'm unlovable, willful, disobedient, and just plain wrong. And thank You, Jesus, for showing your unfathomable love by giving Your life for me. I give You praise, honor, and glory for it all. Hallelujah and Amen."

Week 2
Dashing Relationship
Day 12

*I*ntimacy

Break 2912, You Got Your Ears On? Come Back?

My dad had a CB (Citizens Band) Radio in the 1970s and 1980s. CB radios are personal use transmission systems for person-to-person communication on a high-frequency band. Truck drivers and CB Radio enthusiasts, like my dad, mainly used them.

Dad loved talking on his CB. He would take it out of his truck, set it up in the house, and talk. Then he would take it back to the truck, plug it in, and talk some more; he had his own personal version of a mobile phone. I remember riding with him on the highway listening to his conversations. CBers would exchange information on where to rest and eat, share locations of speed traps, accidents, and construction delays; whatever was needed. They even had their own language, including CB Radio names called handles.

"Then you will call upon me and come and pray to me, and I will hear you" (Jeremiah 29:12, NRSV).

After the 1970s, CB radios became less popular. They were eventually replaced by mobile phones and the Internet. However, my dad continued to use his. Even though they were antiquated, old school, and no longer popular, he always had someone on the other end to talk to.

Prayer is our CB (Christian Band) Radio with a frequency so high that only the children of God can effectively utilize it. When Jesus died, the veil in the temple tore, so we no longer need others to speak for us. We can go directly to God in prayer.

When was the last time you prayed, and how often do you pray? Has prayer become an after-thought? An archaic ritual? God is waiting on the CB to hear from you. He is waiting to converse with you, bless you, and answer your questions and requests. He is waiting to tell you which direction to go, about speed traps, accidents, construction delays, whatever you need.

"Father God, thank You for staying on the CB prayer frequency so that I can speak directly with You. My prayer is that we keep our conversation going along with Jesus until You change my handle and say, 'Well done, good buddy, well done.' In Jesus' name, I pray. Amen."

Week 2
Dashing Relationship
Day 13

Naked

Naked As A J-Bird

My son is an only child. He and I have a great relationship. From the moment he was born, we bonded for life. When he was a toddler, he used to love to take a bath. He would splash around and play with his toys and the bubbles in the water. One time after taking him out of the tub, I was drying him off, and he wiggled away from me and darted out of the bathroom, running around the house laughing and smiling—naked as a Jaybird.

"**Adam and his wife were both naked, and they felt no shame**" (Genesis 2:25, NIV).

Dashing Life Stories

In the American penal system during the 1920s and 1930s, **J-bird** was short for Jailbird. When guards brought inmates in from the bus, they went to the showers, got their kit, and were made to walk from one end of the prison to the other naked, hence, naked as a Jaybird. My son's sprint from the bathroom all around the house is reminiscent of the jailhouse walk with these exceptions: he was not in jail, he was happy, he was free, he was clean, and I was behind him to ensure his safety.

Your relationship with God should be one of authenticity and transparency, where you are naked, stripped of all fear, pretense, guilt, and shame. Jesus died and washed you clean, so you could be happy and free to enjoy an abundant life, knowing He has got your back. Are you presenting yourself naked before God? Is He able to run freely in every area of your life?

God sent Jesus to pay your bail to free you from the jail of sin and death. He saved you so He could freely commune with you. Isn't it time for you to take that long, naked walk back in the other direction and get back on the bus headed to a *Dashing Life*?

"Father God, I come to You naked and unashamed. You knew me before I was born. You know every hair on my head, every freckle, wrinkle, and dimple. You know my fears, faults, hopes, and dreams. Please run freely in every area of my life, clearing the path for me to *dash*. All this I ask in Jesus' name. Amen."

Week 2
Dashing Relationship
Day 14

*G*ratitude

Throw Your Hands In The Air And Praise Him Like You Just Don't Care

When I was in my 20s and early 30s, I loved to party at the club. My friends and I would often start on Wednesday night and party every night until Sunday. It didn't matter how long we had to wait in line, how much it cost, how crowded or smoky it was, nor how much drinks cost. No matter the circumstance, we were just glad to be in "the house." The DJ would often start a call and response chant first coined by Rock Master Scott and the Dynamic Three, which encourages the listener to throw their hands in the air and party without a care. And that is exactly what we did. We kicked it in the club to the wee hours of the night, throwing our hands in the air, and we literally didn't care.

"Enter his gates with thanksgiving, and his courts with praise. Give thanks to him, bless his name. For the Lord is good; his steadfast love endures forever, and his faithfulness to all generations" (Psalms 100:4-5, NRSV).

No matter what was going on, we religiously went clubbing just about every week and were grateful for the opportunity to do it regardless of the circumstances. We outwardly displayed that gratitude with our time, our money, in our conversation, through the songs we sang and other outward expressions that carried over to late-night breakfast and after-hour clubs. It became a lifestyle.

An Attitude of Gratitude is a choice, not just for when all is going well, not only reserved for the church house but carried over and transitioned into a lifestyle. God is the Great I AM. He said and has proven that everything we need and desire, **He is**. Therefore, how can we not give Him glory, honor, thanksgiving, worship, and praise? Do your actions and lifestyle reflect an attitude of gratitude? When was the last time you said, "Thank You, Father, Thank You, Jesus," and truly meant it?

"Father God, thank You for *who you are*! For being the Great, I AM. Thank You for another opportunity to throw my hands in the air to praise and thank You because I know You care. Glory to your name! Hallelujah and Amen."

Week 3
Dashing Growth
Day 15

Develop
Photo Finish

I have a bunch of old photos of family, friends, and special moments. They are priceless to me. I have been told I need to get with the times and digitize them, but I like my old school Polaroids. Since we live in a society of instant gratification, digital pics are the preference, but Polaroids are making a comeback! Polaroids instantly come out of the camera but are distorted and unrecognizable. They need more time to develop.

"But grow in the grace and knowledge of our Lord and Savior Jesus Christ. To him be glory both now and forever! Amen" (2 Peter, 3:18 NIV).

Dashing Life Stories

If you want to speed up the development of a Polaroid picture, the secret is to add a little wind by shaking it. After a short while, you will have a tangible image to hold in your hand that is readily available to be seen, shared, and enjoyed. Spiritual growth and development are essential to having a *Dashing Life*. It is much like the Growth stage in our life cycle in that it requires parental protection and provision, DNA determines our traits, and individual effort is needed to move from infancy and to maturity.

Spiritual immaturity looks like an undeveloped Polaroid, distorted by sin, looking like the world and not like Jesus. Spiritual maturity is the developed Polaroid that can be seen as an image of light in a dark world to be shared and used by God.

What does your spiritual Polaroid currently look like? Do you need more time to develop? Do you need God to shake you to get you going? Or has the breath of God ignited your development? If your Polaroid is distorted and not developed, start putting forth the effort to grow toward maturity. It's already in your DNA, and God is ready with protection and provision for your growth journey.

"Dear Heavenly Father, thank You for providing Jesus as an example of what I should look like. Thank You for giving me the time, tools, and teachers to grow and develop. Thank You for shaking me when I need it and breathing in my direction to give me wings. Thank You for the DNA that grafted me into Your family and made You my Father. I pray that I never take Your grace for granted and that I grow in the knowledge of Your will, Your Word, and Your way. All this I pray in Jesus' name. Amen."

Week 3
Dashing Growth
Day 16

*A*dhere

The Ten Suggestions

I grew up in a household with a brother, a sister, and two loving parents. I knew they loved me because they verbally told and physically showed me in so many ways. One of those ways was providing structure and establishing rules and boundaries such as:

1. Thou shall not talk back.

2. Thou shall respect thine elders.

3. Thou shall stay out of grown folks' business.

4. Thou shall say please and thank you.

5. Thou shall not run in and out of the house.

6. Thou shall not be asked to do something more than once.

7. Thou shall not go out and play until thy homework is done.

8. Thou shall not go out and play until thy chores are done.

9. Thou shall not go out and play until thy bed is made.

10. Thou shall not watch cartoons until thy chores are done.

I rationalized that some of them were more of a suggestion than a hard, fast rule. So, every now and then, I would test those boundaries with varying results. Some results were more successful than others, but at the end of the day, I still knew I was loved and that their rules were for my good. As I grew older, gaining more understanding, I wanted to follow their rules and did so without prompting.

"If you love me, keep my commands" (John 14:15, NIV).

Rules without a relationship lead to regression, rebellion, or both. Like the Ten Commandments Moses received from God, my parents' rules were not suggestions. They started out as "*do as I say*" or "*because I said so*" commands, but because of our relationship, I grew in obedience.

The keys to growing in obedience to God are relationship and faith. When you put your trust in God, you became a new creature with a new nature. That new nature longs to do God's will, and that desire, in response to His love, fuels the relationship. Is your relationship with God growing or regressing? Are you embracing or rebelling against your new nature? Submit in obedience in response to His love, and nature will take its course.

"Father God, I know You do all things for my good. I want our relationship to grow and my new nature to flourish. So, today, I submit to Your will and Your way. Thank You and Amen."

Week 3
Dashing Growth
Day 17

*S*cripture

Sticks And Stones

Kids can be cruel. This I know because I have been on the receiving end of that cruelty. At the beginning of my fourth-grade year, I had an opportunity to skip to fifth-grade or attend Gifted School. My parents choose the latter. Because of this, some neighborhood kids shunned and teased me, saying things like, "You think you are so smart. You think you are so cute. You think you are better than us." Their words hurt just as much as their actions.

"In the beginning was the Word, and the Word was with God, and the Word was God" (John 1:1, NRSV).

"Sticks and stones may break my bones, but words will never hurt me," and "What you don't know can't hurt you" are popular sayings we have all heard. They indicate that words have no power, that knowledge has no power. Not true. God spoke the world into existence with words. He speaks truth, wisdom, and caring to us through the Bible. He saved us with the "Word" made flesh in Jesus. In my case, those kids' words did hurt, but the knowledge I gained in Gifted School allowed me to graduate top of my elementary school class.

God speaks to us through His written Word. It is the most powerful tool we have as Christians and is key to our spiritual growth. It is part love letter and part instruction manual, showing and telling that He loves us and how to live because He knows what is best for us—changing us into His image.

When was the last time you picked up the Bible? Is reading it part of your normal routine? If not, it should be. You need to study it regularly to know what it says and means. You need to memorize it to use when you need comfort, discernment to make wise decisions, a weapon against the enemy, and guidance to deal with the general sticks and stones of life. You also need to regularly hear God's Word to re-enforce your reading so that you have the knowledge and power to live a *Dashing Life*.

"Father God, thank You for the Word and the Word made flesh in Jesus. As I read Your Word, please show me what You

Dashing Growth

want me to see in Your Word, hear in Your Word, learn from Your Word, and do with Your Word. All this I ask in Jesus' name. Amen."

Week 3
Dashing Growth
Day 18

Holy Spirit

We Got Spirit!
Yes We Do!
We Got Spirit!
How About You?

I was the captain of my eighth-grade cheerleading squad. We were school ambassadors appointed by the principal. Our job was to encourage students to tap into the power of school spirit, help them keep it at all times, help them remember who they were so they could act in accordance with that identity, help them to remember and be grateful for what they had been taught in school, and encourage them to beat our opponents. As captain, I had the added responsibility of being an advocate and example for my squad. Unfortunately, that year was not a good year for our sports teams. We lost more games than we won. Our student body needed school spirit more than ever. So, we held a pep rally. One of our go-to cheers was the call and response spirit chant. Time after time, that chant had evoked the power and remembrance that when we have the spirit and let it take over, we could do anything, including win.

"These things I have spoken to you while being present with you. But the Helper, the Holy Spirit, whom the Father will send in My name, He will teach you all things, and bring to your remembrance all things that I said to you" (John 14:25-26, NKJV).

The first pep rally was such a success that the principal gave us the authority to hold one each month. Eventually, the school spirit began to positively change the way we walked, the way we talked, the way we thought, and the way we acted in school, whether we won or not.

The Holy Spirit is the third person in the Godhead like we cheerleaders were to my school's principal and assistant principal. He is our Helper, sent by God until Jesus returns. If we listen to and let the Holy Spirit guide and change us, positive growth will occur. Do you have spirit? Are you listening to the still small voice of the Holy Spirit? Is it as loud as a cheerleading squad, and you

Dashing Growth

still don't hear it? He is speaking to you. Stop, look and listen! Take heed to what He is telling you, and let Him take over. When you do, you can do anything, and you will win.

"Father God, thank You for sending the Holy Spirit to be our Advocate, Comforter, Conscious, and Guide until Jesus returns. Holy Spirit, I pray that You continue to speak to my heart and take over so that I can grow and become all that God has called me to be. I ask this in Jesus' name. Amen."

Week 3
Dashing Growth
Day 19

*I*dentity

Witness Protection Program

One of the popular sayings in the church of my youth was, "Can I get a witness?" The preacher regularly asked this question to see if the congregation was following along and/or agreeing with his message. I sat in the balcony with the rest of the youth, not always paying attention. My mother sang in the choir and sat in the choir box, which was elevated with a direct line of sight to the balcony. My grandmother was a deaconess and always sat on the third row of the sanctuary. Periodically, my mom would scan the balcony to see if I was paying attention. If she saw that I was not, she would wait until she caught my eye and signal me to go downstairs and sit on the third row with my grandmother. Down there, I had no choice but to be a witness. I was too close not to be.

"I have been crucified with Christ; it is no longer I who live, but Christ lives in me; and the life which I now live in the flesh I live by faith in the Son of God, who loved me and gave Himself for me" (Galatians 2:20, NKJV).

By sending me to sit with my grandmother, my mom ensured I was a witness to and gained an understanding of our faith so that I would be covered by the love and protection of God. As a child, I got *voluntold* into the church family but voluntarily stayed in the Body of Christ once I received my identity by knowing Jesus for myself.

Participation in a Federal Witness Protection Program (WPP) is entirely voluntary. After a witness agrees to testify, they become eligible to receive protection. Witnesses and their families receive documentation of a new identity. While witnesses and their family members are free to return to their former identities, they do so at their own risk. God's Witness Protection Program works similarly. Likewise, it is also voluntary. After you confessed and placed your faith in Jesus, your sin nature died with Him, and your new nature rose with Him. That resurrection gave you a new identity in Christ.

Knowing who you are is key to spiritual growth. Once you know, you will increasingly and consistently act accordingly. Have you gone back to your old identity time and time again?

Dashing Growth

How often do you utilize your documentation in the form of the Bible to educate and remind yourself of who you are? By not embracing and living your new identity in Christ, you risk returning to your old sinful self. Isn't it time to embrace your new identity, pay attention to God's calling on your life, grow in that calling, and choose daily to let Christ live in you by faith? If so, can I get a witness?

"Lord Jesus, You gave Your life so that I can have a new life with and through You. That new life is covered and protected by Your blood. Thank You for my new identity and protection. By faith, I will witness to others what You have done, are doing, and will do in my life. I give praise, honor, glory, and blessings to You always. Amen."

Week 3
Dashing Growth
Day 20

Nor'easter

Winds Of Change

I grew up in the Midwest, where I was blessed to experience all four seasons. Spring was storm season. You could always tell a storm was coming by the change in the wind. It would change either in direction, intensity, or velocity, causing floods and tornados with winds so loud you could hear it howling. When it stormed, we were told to get off the phone, turn off the TV, stay away from windows, and get quiet because God was working. Sometimes the lights went off, leaving us sitting in the dark. It was frightening, but after each storm, I would call my friend who lived across the street to meet me outside, and we would take off our shoes and splash barefoot in the puddles.

"Consider it pure joy, my brothers and sisters, whenever you face trials of many kinds, because you know that the testing of your faith produces perseverance. Let perseverance finish its work so that you may be mature and complete, not lacking anything" (James 1:2-4, NIV).

A nor'easter is a storm named for the direction of the wind and the region it usually affects. Weather can move in any direction but typically follows the jet stream from west to east. Therefore, a nor'easter is not your typical storm. Even more atypical is a nor'easter in the Midwest. However, it does happen.

The direction of East is spiritually significant. Each day, the sun rises in the east, signifying a new beginning, new blessings, and new opportunities. God sent an East wind to blow locusts into Egypt as punishment for not freeing Israel and sent an East wind to clear a path for the Israelites to walk through the Red Sea on dry land.

God sends nor'easters in the form of trials, tests, and tribulations that are atypical, made by God just for you. They may or may not be disciplinary, and they either come from God or are allowed by God. Either way, they are used by Him. They are scary, intimidating, and sometimes painful. However, the key is to stay in faith. Storms are sent to grow, teach, or test you in some area of your life. They are meant for your good and His purpose. Remember, after the storm, there is growth, puddles to play in,

Dashing Growth

and rainbows to remind you of the promises of God, which are, "Yes and Amen."

"Dear Father, there is a saying that "we are either heading into a storm, going through a storm or coming out of one." As the Gardener, You are using these storms to continually prune, nurture, and grow us. Thank You for my storms filled with love, purpose, and possibilities. I give You praise, honor, and glory for them all. In Jesus' name. Amen."

Week 3
Dashing Growth
Day 21

Grace

The Gift That Keeps On Giving

I had a baby at age 18. I found out I was pregnant in an unusual and dramatic way. I was in a bad car accident. Our car hit a highway bridge, went airborne, landed on its roof, and caught fire. I was not wearing a seatbelt at the time. After the accident, I was given a routine pregnancy test in the ER before being sent to Radiology for a brain scan; the test result was positive. I was disappointed and mad at myself. I thought my parents felt the same. I was wrong. Their reaction was just the opposite. Thankful I was alive, they gave me the love, kindness, and grace I didn't deserve and couldn't give myself.

"In Him we have redemption through His blood, the forgiveness of sins, according to the riches of His grace" (Ephesians 1:7, NKJV).

God, through His infinite grace and mercy, gave us Jesus. He gave His life to save us from sin and death. Jesus also saved me and my son's life that day. As my son grew and made missteps, I gave him grace like my parents had given me. I also gave and still give grace to others whom I encounter in my life. I taught my son to do the same.

God's grace is free and unmerited. It channels His love and kindness. It is all that He can and will do for us through the work of Jesus on our behalf that we don't deserve and cannot do for ourselves. We cannot earn it, and we cannot repay it. However, we can pay it forward. Growing in grace is to mature in your knowledge of and relationship with Jesus Christ. As you do so, you will look and act more like Jesus and less like the world.

Grace creates an atmosphere for spiritual growth. However, that atmosphere does not shield you from growing pains, hurts, trials, or tribulations. In those situations, God may not take away your challenge, but He will give you the grace to endure.

Your response to God's grace depends on your spiritual maturity level. Is your knowledge of and relationship with Christ such that you can be thankful regardless of the situation? Such that you are ready for service and ready to pay it forward? If not, think about where you are now, where you came from, and how you got here. I don't know about you, but I know how I survived a deadly car accident, raised a healthy child, finished college, have a successful career, and became a published author. It was all through God's grace. So, I can't help but praise Him, serve Him, and pay it forward. What about you?

"Father God and Lord Jesus, thank You for Your grace, mercy, and loving-kindness towards me. I pray that You continue to provide me with an atmosphere to grow in Your grace and pay it forward. In Jesus' name, I pray. Amen."

# Week 4
Dashing Purpose
Day 22

Decrease
Tweener Blues

I am currently considered a tweener. A tweener is a word I use to describe a stage in my life where I'm in the middle, and something about me must decrease so something else can increase—thus the term tweener. I have been a "tweener" several times in my life. First, at age 12, I was in between pre-teen and full-fledged teenager. Around age 20, I was not a teenager but wasn't legally considered an adult until age 21. In my mid to late 30s, I was in between young adult and midlife. Now I'm in between midlife and senior. This stage, like my others, is not easy. Like the previous ones, I am too young to be old and too old to be young. Fifty is not the new 40! I'm not sure if this is a mid-life crisis, but it's giving me the blues.

"He must increase, but I must decrease" (John 3:30, NKJV).

Often, as tweeners, we are holding on to the old while reaching out for the new. We want the comfort of the familiar and the benefits of change. When I was in my 20s, I lived with my parents for a few years rent-free. Those were also my party years, so we often disagreed on my weekend curfew. I wanted to keep my money and live by my rules but in their house. For me to increase the freedom of adulthood, my childish ways had to decrease, which meant moving out on my own.

Biblical tweener choices are usually polar opposites, such as good and evil, heaven and hell, or life and death. These opposites often result in a crisis that requires a decision.

The **dash** between your birth date and your heavenly return date is another in-between. This in-between is your life, your calling, and your purpose. The only way for you to find God's purpose for your in-between is for you to decrease so that He can increase. You can do that by spending time with Him in study, prayer, and meditation, as well as spending time with others in the Body of Christ, where you hold one another accountable and pray and fight for and with each other. As you do, you will find the in-between gets easier, and you will move from crisis to Christ-like.

Dashing Purpose

"Lord Jesus, thank You for guiding and loving me through all my past tweener stages. Please continue to do the same in this stage as I shape my **dash** in Your image to fulfill my purpose for Your Kingdom. I ask this in your precious name. Amen."

Week 4
Dashing Purpose
Day 23

*A*uthority
VIP Seating

If you ask my family, they will say I am spoiled, and I agree. Because I am used to be being "pampered," I expect and often get VIP seats for concerts, plays, and other performances, as well as first-class seats on flights. In April 2016, a friend and I went to see *Motown the Musical*. A friend-of-a-friend had a friend in the cast, and the cast member got us aisle seats on the floor, 4th row. Unbeknownst to me, mine was the perfect seat to become part of the play.

In one of the Acts, Diana Ross' character was doing a concert, and we were her audience. She asked for volunteers to sing with her, and I raised my hand. Then one of the Temptations came off stage, extended his hand to me, helped me get out of my seat, and escorted me to join Diana Ross. She asked me my name, and we had a little banter. She then put her arm around me and asked if I was ready to sing. I said, "Yes," and she sang one verse of "Reach Out and Touch" and then turned the mic to me. I repeated the same verse, and we went on from there. That seat gave me the opportunity and authority to join the cast and command that stage. It would not have happened if I was sitting in a different seat.

"And God raised us up with Christ and seated us with him in the heavenly realms in Christ Jesus" (Ephesians 2:6, NIV).

After the play, as I was walking out, several people came up to me to tell me how good I was. Some expressed that they thought I was an audience plant and part of the cast. When I told them I was not, they said I was brave, a natural on stage, and a good singer. Because of the connection I had with a friend-of-a-friend, I discovered hidden talents, bravery, and courage I did not know I had.

When you gave your life to Christ, your old self died, and God raised up your new self and seated you in heavenly places. The word "seated" is past tense, meaning it's already done. You are living on earth, but your true self is in heaven seated next to Jesus, who is seated at the right hand of God. Jesus is that friend-of-a-friend who has the power and connection for whatever you want and need. Because of your VIP seat, through Jesus, you have an opportunity to explore your gifts, talents, and authority to take your seat and do your **dash**.

"Lord Jesus, thank You for seating me in a position of authority. I do not take for granted the price You paid to put me here. You are the author of my authority, and as such, please edit and format me in Your image so that others will see You in me and in my *dash*. I pray this in Your matchless name. Amen."

Week 4
Dashing Purpose
Day 24

Serve

CrossWord Puzzle

I have never really been a puzzle person, crossword, jigsaw, or otherwise. That all changed when I decided to create one myself. I work in Human Resources and was tasked with creating training on a boring compliance topic. I wanted the training to be informative, interactive, thought-provoking, and fun. I decided to do an exercise that was a cross between the TV game shows "Wheel of Fortune" and "Jeopardy." However, crafting it was not as easy as I imagined. The clues had to be challenging but not so difficult that no one could guess the answers. The same went for the square spacing and coordination of available squares versus unavailable squares. The number of words and squares had to be precise, and the entire puzzle had to have an overall theme relevant for the training.

"For I have given you an example, that you should do as I have done to you" (John 13:15, NKJV).

Who doesn't like a good crossword puzzle? They are a great way to exercise your mind and pass the time. They can be easy or frustrating. It all depends on your understanding of the clues provided and discernment of the placement of open squares horizontally and vertically so that the intersection forms parts of two words.

The Cross of Jesus represents many things; one of them is the *vertical relationship* between us here on earth and God in heaven. The other is the *horizontal relationship* we have with each other. Jesus is at the center, intersecting the two.

Are you vertically vexed or horizontally hindered? Are you having difficulty discerning the deliberate spacing in your life that solves the CrossWord puzzle of your purpose? If so, Jesus is the answer. He is the Word made flesh. He is the ultimate example of serving the Father vertically and others horizontally. He has the answers to the closed and open doors that solve your purpose puzzle. His sacrifice on the cross affords you the "Wheel of Fortune" prize of eternal life, saving your soul from "Jeopardy." So, isn't it time to stop playing games? Your service is needed.

"Lord Jesus, You said in Mark 10:45, NIV, "For the Son of Man came not to be served but to serve." Thank you for being the

Dashing Purpose

example of service to our Heavenly Father and my earthly neighbors. Please help me solve my CrossWord puzzle so my ***dash*** can serve the purpose You have for me. I ask this in your glorious name. Amen."

Week 4
Dashing Purpose
Day 25

*H*istory

I Have No Spades And Only One Face Card

I love to play Spades. For those of you who have never heard of it, Spades is a popular card game where three to four players compare cards one at a time, and the highest valued card wins the others. The spade cards are the highest valued and usually win. However, face cards are also highly valued. You can ask for a re-deal if you are dealt no spades and no face cards. Otherwise, you play the hand you are dealt. I remember one game, in particular, where I had no spades and one face card. It is one of the worst hands you can get. To a novice player, this would have been a problem. However, I consider myself a Spadologist, which means that due to my history and experience, I knew how to play and play well. The outcome of the game was typical for a Spadologist. We won, but how?

[34] "But David said to Saul, "Your servant has been keeping his father's sheep. When a lion or a bear came and carried off a sheep from the flock, I went after it, struck it, and rescued the sheep from its mouth. When it turned on me, I seized it by its hair, struck it, and killed it."

[49] "Reaching into his bag and taking out a stone, he slung it and struck the Philistine on the forehead. The stone sank into his forehead, and he fell face down on the ground. So, David triumphed over the Philistine with a sling and a stone; without a sword in his hand, he struck down the Philistine and killed him" (1 Samuel 17:34-35, 49-50).

One other thing I forgot to mention about Spades is that in a four-person game, you have partners. Whatever my hand lacked, my partner picked up the slack. The combination of history and partnership made us unbeatable regardless of the hand that I was dealt.

David was the youngest and smallest of eight boys. His older brothers fought battles while he tended sheep. However, tending sheep sometimes meant facing fierce opposition. His victories against that opposition prepared him for his battle with Goliath. David's victory over Goliath was part of God's plan for his journey to becoming King of Israel.

Dashing Purpose

Do you have a passion due to something in your history? Have you acted on it? If not, why? Are you fearful? Do you feel inadequate? Don't forget you have a partner. God is your partner in this game of life. Like David, God has equipped you for your purpose through your past experiences. You will do more than you can imagine, even with a sling and some stones or no spades and one face card.

"Father God, You use all things for my good and for Your purpose. Please give me revelation to see Your guiding hand in my *Dashing Journey*, knowing that, with You, I will do more than I can imagine. In Jesus' name, I pray. Amen."

Week 4
Dashing Purpose
Day 26

*I*ncubation

The WIIFM In The Wait

I graduated high school after my junior year. I was bored, cutting class, and hanging with the wrong crowd. My parents and the Dean of Girls thought it would be best that I graduate early. Therefore, I graduated in May of my junior year and went straight to my first college summer session in June. Even though I was book-smart, I was still an emotionally immature 17-year-old. As a result, I was placed in a new student incubator program, where I had time over the summer to prepare for college life. I thought it would be one big party, but it was not. My fellow cohorts and

I had targeted classes with assigned mentors, tutors, and college prep assignments. I could not wait to go to college, but I was immature and ill-prepared. That program gave me what I needed when I needed it, even though I didn't know I needed it. I didn't know the WIIFM (What's In It For Me) in the wait.

"To everything there is a season, a time for every purpose under heaven" (Ecclesiastes 3:1, NKJV).

Incubation is the act of maintaining controlled environmental conditions for the purpose of growth or development; to keep something at the right temperature and under the right conditions favoring that development and growth. In medical terms, it is the time from the moment of exposure to an infectious agent until the appearance of signs and symptoms. Had I gone straight to college without that program, as immature as I was, I might have again fallen in with the wrong crowd. Though I was ready to skip the incubation process, God was not.

You have a God-given purpose. However, the promise of that purpose does not allow you to skip the process of preparation. Any preparation process requires patience, commitment, and time. Do you have the patience and dedication to wait until you are prepared to receive that promise? If so, are you partnering with God and your cohort believers to navigate the process? Are you showing signs and symptoms of that partnership? If you are in your pre-purpose incubation, all these things should be occurring.

Dashing Purpose

Please do not rush the process. What God has for you is for you, and no amount of time will change that. Blessings flowing from your purpose will chase you down. You will show signs and symptoms that you have spent time with Jesus for the purpose of spreading His message to others wherever you go.

"Father God, thank You for my pre-purpose preparation period. I pray that my incubation time with You and Yours makes me so contagious that everyone I come in contact with will be blessed. All this ask in Jesus' name. Amen."

Week 4
Dashing Purpose
Day 27

Next Chapter
Cliff Notes And A Cliff Hanger

Until just recently, I struggled with having patience. I wanted and felt I needed everything right away. Even when I read a book, I lacked the patience to read chapter-by-chapter and not skip ahead to the end. I was introduced to CliffsNotes in college. Like many students, instead of using them as a study guide as intended, I used them as a substitute. When I couldn't get the CliffsNotes, I would borrow notes from a friend or see the movie version if there was one. These substitutes worked for me all through college, so I got into the habit of taking shortcuts.

Dashing Life Stories

Taking those shortcuts developed into impatience that sometimes came close to being rude.

"For I know the plans I have for you," declares the Lord, "plans to prosper you and not to harm you, plans to give you hope and a future" (Jeremiah 29:11, NIV).

Taking shortcuts and peeking ahead not only fueled my impatience, but it also fueled my intolerance for uncertainty. This intolerance became more apparent as a single parent in my 30s. I was not anxious, but I had to have all bases covered. I needed a plan A, B, C, and D for every scenario in my life. Not knowing my short and long-term future was not an option.

There are quite a few quotes about the importance of the destination versus the journey. The Bible shows both are important. On my path to being more patient, God put me in situations requiring patience that I would have never imagined. There were no shortcuts to allow me to jump to the end.

On your journey to your purpose, are you looking for shortcuts? Are you planning the destination and the path to take to get there? God has plans for you that you can't do on your own nor the mental capacity to fathom. However, you can't take shortcuts. Every mile of your journey has a purpose. Get in agreement with God today to walk with Him and trust His way. You will find the Cliff at the end is overlooking your destiny.

"Father God, Your plans are what's best for me. Thank You that no matter how many shortcuts I try to take, it does not short circuit Your plan for my life. Help me to trust You more and question You less. I ask this in Jesus' name. Amen."

Week 4
Dashing Purpose
Day 28

Gifts

If The Present Fits, I Must Re-Gift

My friends and family tease me about my gift closet. It contains things I have received and didn't like or that didn't physically fit me or my personality. To keep from hurting the giver's feelings, I put these items in my gift closet and save them for someone better suited for the gift. Some may think that re-gifting is thoughtless and cheap. However, I feel it is thoughtful and smart. It's smart because I don't spend money unnecessarily. It's thoughtful because I don't hurt the feelings of the original giver nor, in most cases, waste their money. I put thought into every item I re-gift. Consequently, some have been in my closet so long they must be repurposed or thrown out. I strive for the perfect fit. If not, I won't commit. If so, I must re-gift.

"We have different gifts, according to the grace given to each of us" (Roman 12:6, NIV).

Whether I am in a store, online, or in my gift closet when I shop, the item must speak to me. I use my senses (sight, smell, and touch) to discern its exact match. If I don't spend time with it, I won't recognize the owner, which could cause someone to miss their blessing.

God also has a gift closet. Unlike my closet, where there are unspecified unassigned gifts, His has blessings, gifts, and talents with your name on them. However, like mine, timing is everything. You have to spend time with God: spend time with Him in prayer; spend time reading and studying His Word to learn what He has for you and apply it to your life so that He can recognize you.

Spending quality time with Him will enable you to discern your gift(s). You also have to wait on His perfect timing. You can't move too late or too soon. Lastly, you must be present while you are waiting. Being present means no matter what is going on in your life, you are not waiting passively, expecting God to come to you. You must move faithfully in His direction so that you receive your gift(s) at the right time and place.

Like my closet, if the gift is not redeemed, it will be lost. But once redeemed, use it or lose it. God does not gift us just for ourselves; He gifts us to serve others. We are stewards of these gifts,

Dashing Purpose

which means the owner (God) can take them away at any time, especially if we are not using them. Are your gifts sitting in the heavenly gift closet unredeemed? Are you allowing them to get moldy or dusty? Are they nearly out of style or no longer useful? Do what is necessary to discover, redeem and use your gifts today. For today is your first gift. That is why it is called the present.

"Father God, thank You for talents, blessings, and gifts made just for me. I want to be a good steward of them. Please show me what, when, where, and how I should use them. All this I ask in the mighty name of Jesus. Amen."

Week 5
Dashing Forward
Day 29

Dash

White Knuckles And A Tailwind

I used to be deathly afraid of flying. I was so afraid that back then, if you had looked up the term "white knuckler" in a dictionary, you might have seen a picture of me. I avoided flying at all costs. Those costs included missing events, taking more vacation time to offset drive time, being exhausted after a long drive, and using rest stops that were less than optimal, to name a few. At some point, those costs got to be too much. If I wanted to achieve the success and happiness I was seeking from travel, I had to get on a plane.

My first white knuckle experience was so bad that the flight attendants gave me special attention. One sat in front of me on the jump seat and talked with me to keep me occupied. Another gave me free alcoholic beverages and a shoulder massage. (*I told you I was spoiled.*) I was so afraid of dying in a plane crash that I could not enjoy the ride even while getting a drunken massage.

"Most assuredly, I say to you, unless a grain of wheat falls into the ground and dies, it remains alone; but if it dies, it produces much grain. He who loves his life will lose it, and he who hates his life in this world will keep it for eternal life. If anyone serves Me, let him follow Me; and where I am, there My servant will be also. If anyone serves Me, him My Father will honor" (John 12:24-26, NKJV).

I got over my fear of flying by learning everything there was to know about it, such as a bell rings at 10,000 feet to let the flight attendants know everything is okay; clouds make the flight bumpy, although you can have clear air turbulence, and headwinds slow the plane down while tailwinds speed it up.

We all want to go to heaven, but few want to die. Everyone wants Success and Happiness, but few want to sacrifice. Our society demands instant, and those who wait are few. Life is literally a *dash*. It's quick, short, painful, impactful, beautiful, and finite. If you want to live with Jesus and the Father in the afterlife, you must die in this life, figuratively and literally.

Are you ready to die to self and the flesh to follow Jesus? Are you ready to seek and wait for your purpose in order to achieve the success and happiness that God predestined for you?

Dashing Forward

Like I did with flying, learning all you can through His Word about how to live your *dash* and spending time with Him will remove any fears and give you a tailwind forward.

"Lord Jesus, You taught us through Your life, death, and resurrection the how and why of living and dying. Help me to follow Your example and be that needed tailwind for someone else's *dash*. All this I ask in Your precious and mighty name. Amen."

Week 5
Dashing Forward
Day 30

*I*ng

Verb

In elementary school, I learned a noun is a person, place, or thing, and a verb is an action word. My lessons were reinforced by the School House Rock vignettes on Saturday mornings. Each vignette has a catchy theme song and a main character that depicted a specific educational topic. I especially liked *"Verb"* because he was a Black Superhero. He sang about taking a noun and bending it into a *verb* by adding *"ing,"* which made it actionable and powerful.

"Ask and it will be given to you; seek and you will find; knock and the door will be opened to you" (Matthew 7:7, NIV).

Because schoolwork came easy to me, I developed a habit of procrastination. I would wait until the last minute to do my homework, study for a test, or complete an assignment. The ironic thing is my procrastination is a verb describing inaction. Things coming easily to me also caused me to shy away from things I did not know or do well.

The *dash* in *dashing* represents your life. The only one you have. You can't go back to yesterday, and tomorrow is not promised. Therefore, today is all you have. What are you doing with your *dash* right now? Is it a noun or a *verb*? What's stopping you from adding *"ing"* (IN God), bending it, and sending it out into the world to meet the needs of others, giving God glory, and being the superhero of faith God has called you to be? Stop procrastinating. Stop shying away from things you don't know or do well. Seek Him out, knock on His door, and ask. He has everything you need.

Keep deciding. Keep praying. Keep studying. Keep growing. Keep asking. Keep seeking. Keep knocking until you get your blessing and your calling. In other words, Keep Dashing...

"Father God, I know You will open the door when I knock. I ask for Your grace and guidance as I seek what Your will is for my life. I ask this in the name of Jesus Christ, my risen Lord and Savior. Amen."

About the Author

Elesha Storey is a passionate creative who has turned her passion into a movement inspiring the world through apparel, music, books, media, and conferences to start *Dashing*. After losing her father in 2015, she re-evaluated her life and found her purpose. God turned tragedy into victory when He dropped DASHING (Dying to Achieve Success and Happiness IN God) into her spirit. She has one son and is also a Human Resources leader who is an active member of her church in Plano, Texas. Elesha's mission is to spread the Gospel of Jesus Christ, inspiring and equipping others to find and embrace their purpose and abundant life *in God*.

For more information on the DASHING Movement, visit www.dashingnation.org.